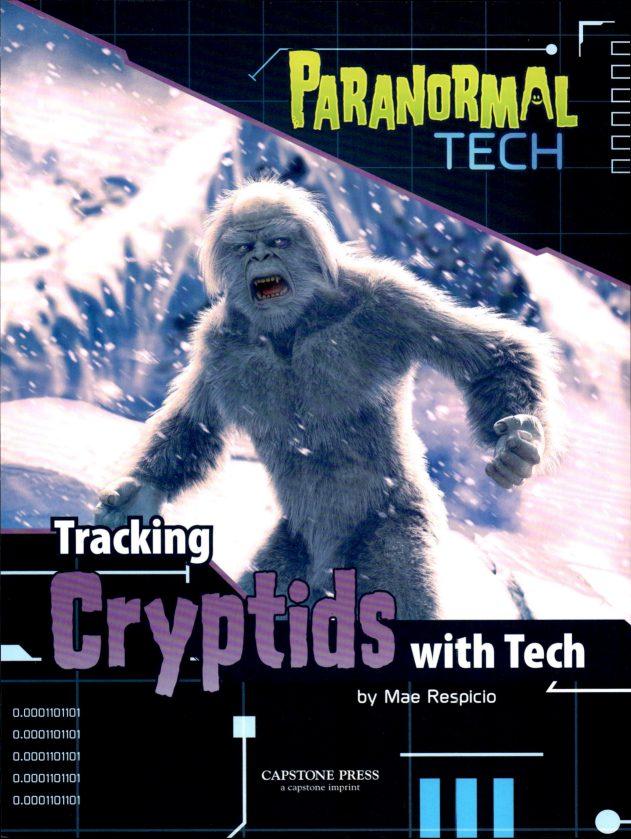

PARANORMAL TECH

Tracking Cryptids with Tech

by Mae Respicio

CAPSTONE PRESS
a capstone imprint

Published by Spark, an imprint of Capstone
1710 Roe Crest Drive
North Mankato, Minnesota 56003
capstonepub.com

Copyright © 2024 by Capstone. All rights reserved. No part of this publication may be reproduced in whole or in part, or stored in a retrieval system, or transmitted in any form or by any means, electronic, mechanical, photocopying, recording, or otherwise, without written permission of the publisher.

Library of Congress Cataloging-in-Publication Data is available on the Library of Congress website.
ISBN: 9781669049753 (hardcover)
ISBN: 9781669049715 (ebook PDF)

Summary: Reports of Bigfoot, the Loch Ness monster, and other cryptids come from all over the world. Could they be true? Get an inside look at all the high-tech gear people use to hunt for elusive cryptids, including sonar, night-vision goggles, and drones.

Editorial Credits
Editor: Carrie Sheely; Designer: Jaime Willems; Media Researcher: Rebekah Hubstenberger; Production Specialist: Whitney Schaefer

Image Credits
Alamy: REUTERS/Eriko Sugita, 27; Associated Press: Shannon Roae/Meadville Tribune, 19; Getty Image: Anastasiia Krivenok, 26, Ernst Haas, 25, iStock, cover (thermal imager), iStock/Milan Krasula, 21, Jeff J Mitchell, 11, Keystone, 8, Patrick T. Fallon/Bloomberg, 17, TEK IMAGE/SCIENCE PHOTO LIBRARY, 24, VICTOR HABBICK VISIONS/SCIENCE PHOTO LIBRARY, 5; Shutterstock Premier: Peter Jolly, 13; Shutterstock: CreativeHQ, 18, Daniel Eskridge, 15, 28, Fer Gregory, 6, George KUZ, 7, Oliver Denker, 1, 23, ozbayemrah, 10, Stefano Dosselli, cover (background), Teri Virbickis, 14, Unique Vision, cover (yeti)

Design Elements: Shutterstock: alleachday, Tex vector, ZinetroN

All internet sites appearing in back matter were available and accurate when this book was sent to press.

Printed and bound in China. PO5379

Table of Contents

Are Cryptids Real? 4
Looking for the Loch Ness Monster 6
Searching for Bigfoot 14
Tracking the Yeti 22
Cryptids and Technology 26
    Glossary 30
    Read More 31
    Internet Sites 31
    Index 32
    About the Author 32

Words in bold are in the glossary.

Are Cryptids Real?

The Loch Ness Monster. Bigfoot. Yeti. Maybe you have heard stories about these creatures. They are called **cryptids**.

Are cryptids real? People around the world use many tools to find out. See how **technology** is hot on the trail of cryptids!

Fact:
Cryptozoologists are people who study cryptids.

The Yeti is said to live in the snowy mountains of Asia.

Looking for the Loch Ness Monster

One of the most famous cryptids is the Loch Ness Monster. It is also known as Nessie. It is said to live in a lake in Scotland called Loch Ness.

Many reports say the Loch Ness Monster has a long, thin body.

People faked the 1934 photo of the Loch Ness Monster using a toy submarine.

Nessie became famous from a picture taken in 1934. It showed a creature. It had a long neck. Was it real? No. It was a **hoax**. But it made people want to search for Nessie.

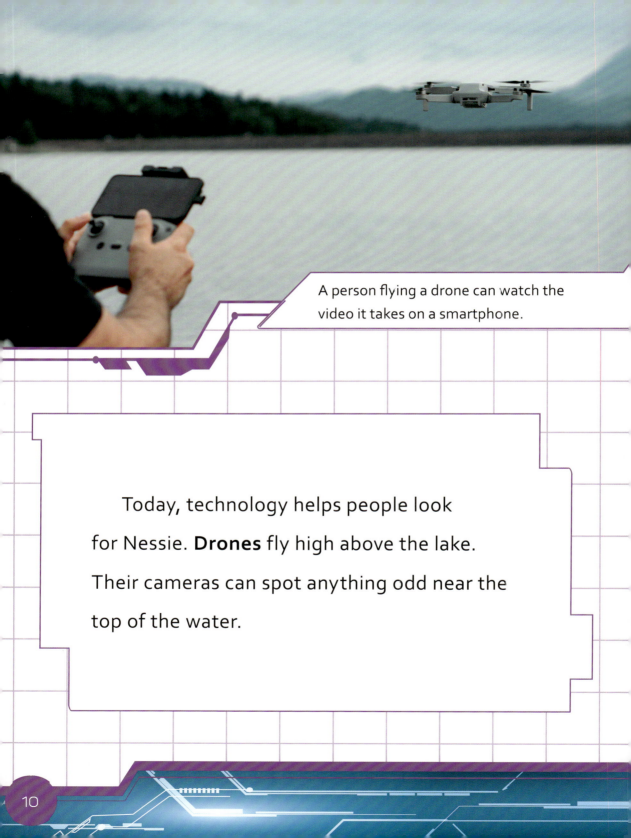

A person flying a drone can watch the video it takes on a smartphone.

Today, technology helps people look for Nessie. **Drones** fly high above the lake. Their cameras can spot anything odd near the top of the water.

Sonar uses sound waves to find objects underwater. It has found many shapes in the same parts of the lake. This tells people where to focus their searches.

A person uses a robot with sonar in Loch Ness.

Once, a team thought they found Nessie using sonar. But the object was fake. It was a **prop** of Nessie from an old movie. The prop had sunk.

Older sonar could easily find shapes on the lake bottom. But it didn't find objects in the water as well. Today's sonar can find objects at all depths. Could it help find Nessie?

Fact:
Stories of the Loch Ness Monster go back to ancient times. One story about Nessie dates back to 565 CE.

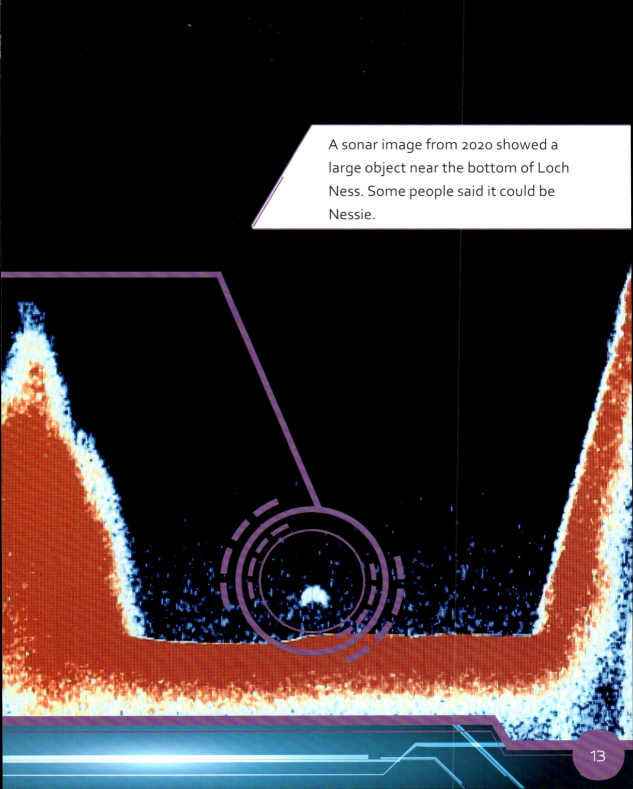

A sonar image from 2020 showed a large object near the bottom of Loch Ness. Some people said it could be Nessie.

Searching for Bigfoot

In the 1950s, loggers in California found strange footprints. Huge ones. They were 16 inches (41 centimeters) long! This is how Bigfoot got its name. It is also known as Sasquatch.

Bigfoot is said to be tall, hairy, and smelly. It walks on two legs like a person. Bigfoot is said to live mainly in North America. It hides in thick forests of the Northwest.

How do people track Bigfoot in a huge forest? Cameras can help. High-quality drone cameras can spot Bigfoot's shelters and nests.

People look for clues in forests. Once something is found, **3D** scanners can take pictures of it. People study the photos up close. They might look at the length and foot arch of footprints. They decide if a print could be from Bigfoot.

A person uses a 3D scanner on a smartphone.

Night-vision goggles

Infrared equipment and night-vision goggles track Bigfoot too. These tools see in the dark. They look for light that people cannot see.

Bigfoot hunter T.J. Biscardi holds an infrared viewer (left).

Fact:
Researchers on a Bigfoot TV show used technology to study 50 years of Bigfoot sightings. It helped them decide where to look for Bigfoot.

Screech! Howl! Bigfoot is said to make loud noises. People try to pick up these noises with sound recorders.

People hide trail cameras in forests too. They hope these cameras will spot Bigfoot.

Trail camera

Fact
Bigfoot hunters use speakers to blast calls into forests. They hope Bigfoot will return the calls.

Tracking the Yeti

Stories of Yeti go farther back in time than those of Bigfoot. People say Yeti lives high in the Himalayan mountains of Asia. It is said to be tall and hairy. Like Bigfoot, Yeti walks on two legs.

Bigfoot's hair is said to be brown. But stories say Yeti's hair can be brown, white, or gray.

People have found teeth, bones, and hair in places Yeti is said to live. Were they from a real Yeti? People tested **DNA** in those items to find out.

DNA is found in **cells**. It carries information about all living things. But DNA from Yeti was not in these items. Much of it was linked to bears.

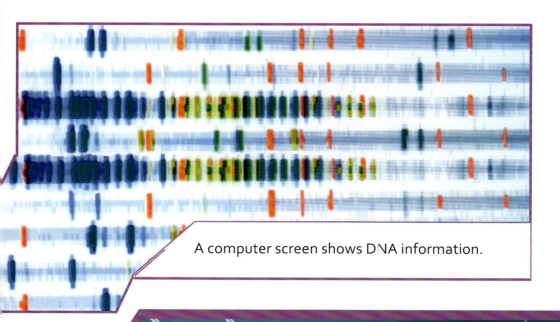

A computer screen shows DNA information.

Fact:
A monastery in Nepal has a partial skull and hand bones said to be from Yeti.

Cryptids and Technology

Most of the time, cryptid hunters find little of interest on searches. But sometimes technology pays off big. People once thought the giant squid was a cryptid. In 2004, photos showed the animals were real.

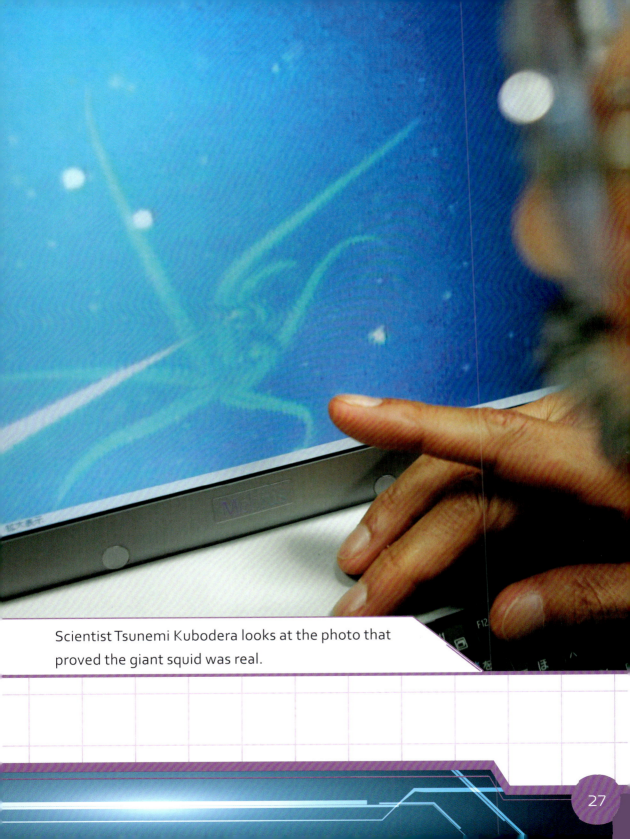

Scientist Tsunemi Kubodera looks at the photo that proved the giant squid was real.

A winged cryptid called the Jersey Devil is said to live in southern New Jersey.

The internet can help cryptid hunters. They use map **apps** on phones. They get ideas of where to look. People can share tips with others on **blogs**.

Could some cryptids be real? No one knows. But people will keep using cutting-edge tech to find out. Do you think they'll ever find **proof**?

Glossary

3D (THREE-DEE)—having length, width, and height; 3D stands for three-dimensional

app (AP)—a program that performs a certain task, usually on a phone

blog (BLOG)—an online journal

cell (SEL)—the smallest unit of a living thing

cryptid (KRIP-tid)—an animal that has been claimed to exist but never proven to exist

DNA (dee-en-AY)—material in cells that gives people their individual characteristics; DNA stands for deoxyribonucleic acid

drone (DROHN)—an unmanned, remote-controlled aircraft

hoax (HOHKS)—an act that is meant to trick people

infrared (in-fruh-RED)—a type of light that is invisible to human eyes

sonar (SOH-nar)—a device that uses sound waves to find underwater objects; sonar stands for sound navigation and ranging

proof (PROOF)—facts or evidence that something is true

prop (PROP)—an item used by an actor or performer during a show

technology (tek-NOL-uh-jee)—the use of science to do practical things

Read More

Colson, Mary. *Bigfoot and Yeti: Myth or Reality?* North Mankato, MN: Capstone, 2019.

Pearson, Marie. *Loch Ness Monster.* North Mankato, MN: Capstone, 2020.

Ransom, Candice F. *Legendary Bigfoot.* Minneapolis: Lerner Publications, 2021.

Internet Sites

Kiddle: Cryptozoology Facts for Kids
kids.kiddle.co/Cryptozoology

Sound Waves Underwater: The Loch Ness Monster
tpt.pbslearningmedia.org/resource/phy03.sci.phys.mfw.lochness/sound-waves-underwater-the-loch-ness-monster/?student=true

Wonderopolis: What Is Cryptozoology?
wonderopolis.org/wonder/What-Is-Cryptozoology

Index

3D scanners, 16

apps, 29

Bigfoot, 4, 14, 15, 16, 18, 19, 20, 21, 22
blogs, 29
bones, 24, 25

cameras, 10, 16, 20

DNA, 24
drones, 10, 16

footprints, 14, 16

giant squid, 26, 27

Loch Ness Monster, 4, 6, 8, 9, 10, 12, 13

Nessie. *See* Loch Ness Monster
night-vision goggles, 18

photos, 8, 16, 26, 27
props, 12

Sasquatch. *See* Bigfoot
sonar, 11, 12, 13
sound recorders, 20
speakers, 21

trail cameras, 20

Yeti, 4, 22, 24

About the Author

Mae Respicio is a nonfiction writer and middle grade author whose books include *The House That Lou Built*, which won an Asian Pacific American Libraries Association honor award and was an NPR Best Book. Mae lives with her family in northern California. Visit her at maerespicio.com.